Hist Whist

Poems of magic and mystery, witches and ghosts

Collected by Dennis Saunders
Illustrated by Kathy Wyatt

Evans

Evans Brothers Limited,
London

Published by Evans Brothers Limited
Montague House, Russell Square,
London, WC1

Set in 11 on 12 point Baskerville
Printed in Great Britain by Butler & Tanner Ltd
Frome and London

ISBN 0 237 44835 1   PRA 4387

Contents

For Violet and Cyril Engledow, with love.

Acknowledgments

For permission to reproduce copyright material, the Editor and Publishers are indebted to the authors and the following:

Abelard-Schumann Ltd: 'All Hallowe'en' by Pauline Clark; George Allen and Unwin Ltd: 'The Mewlips' and 'Shadow-Bride' by J. R. R. Tolkien from *The Adventures of Tom Bombadil*; Coward, McCann & Geoghegan Inc.: 'Daniel Webster's Horses' by Elizabeth Coatsworth from *The Creaking Stair*, copyright 1923 by Elizabeth Coatsworth, copyright 1929, 1949 by Coward-McCann Inc.; Dennis Dobson Publishers: 'Hallowe'en' by Leonard Clark from *Good Company*; Gerald Duckworth & Co Ltd: 'The Changeling' by Charlotte Mew from *Collected Poems*; Faber and Faber Ltd: 'The Silent Eye' by Ted Hughes from *The Earth Owl and other Moon People*, 'Song of the Ogres' by W. H. Auden from *City without Walls and Other Poems* and 'Dinky' by Theodore Roethke from *The Collected Poems of Theodore Roethke*; Robert Graves: 'The *Alice Jean*' from *The Penny Fiddle*, 'The Two Witches' and 'Traveller's Curse after Misdirection' from *The Collected Poems 1965*; Hamish Hamilton Children's Books Ltd: 'Haunted' by William Mayne from *Ghosts*; George G. Harrap & Company Ltd: 'The Ghosts' Walk' by John Kendall; William Heinemann Ltd: 'Queer Things' and 'Old Moll' by James Reeves from *The Wandering Moon* and 'The Snitterjipe' by James Reeves from *Prefabulous Animiles*; Michael Joseph Ltd: 'The Witch, the Witch' by Eleanor Farjeon from *Silver Sand and Snow*; Little, Brown & Co: 'A Spell for Sleeping' by Alastair Reid from *Ounce, Dice, Trice*; James McGibbon: 'The Little Boy Lost' by Stevie Smith; McGibbon & Kee: 'hist whist' by e. e. cummings from *The Complete Poems of e. e. cummings*; Mrs George Bambridge, Macmillan of London & Basingstoke and Macmillan Co of Canada: 'The Way Through the Woods' by Rudyard Kipling from *Rewards and Fairies*; M. B. Yeats, Miss Anne Yeats, Macmillan of London and Basingstoke and Macmillan Co of Canada: 'The Song of Wandering Aengus' by W. B. Yeats from *The Collected Poems of W. B. Yeats*; Methuen & Co Ltd: 'Mixed Brew' and 'The Witches' Call' by Clive Sansom from *The Golden Unicorn*; Anthony Sheil Associates Ltd and Hutchinson & Co (Publishers) Ltd: 'The Emperors of the Island' by Dannie Abse from *Tenants of the House*; The Literary Trustees of Walter de la Mare and the Society of Authors as their representative: 'I Saw Three Witches', 'Bewitched' and 'The Witch' by Walter de la Mare; Ann Wolfe: 'Green Candles' by Humbert Wolfe; World's Work Ltd: 'The Empty House' by Russell Hoban from *The Pedalling Man*. Chatto and Windus Educational Ltd: 'Prince Kano' by Edward Lowbury from *Green Magic*.

Every effort has been made to trace the owners of copyrights, but we take this opportunity of tendering apologies to any owners whose rights may have been unwittingly infringed.

"Bearded Cloaked and and Cowled, They Go...."

Now the Hungry Lion Roars

Now the hungry lion roars
   And the wolf behowls the moon:
Whilst the heavy ploughman snores,
   All with weary task fordone.
Now the wasted brands do glow,
   Whilst the screech-owl, screeching loud,
Puts the wretch that lies in woe
   In remembrance of a shroud.
Now it is the time of night,
   That the graves, all gaping wide,
Every one lets forth his sprite,
   In the churchway paths to glide:
And we fairies, that do run
   By the triple Hecate's team,
From the presence of the sun,
   Following darkness like a dream,
Now are frolic.

William Shakespeare

All Hallowe'en

Witch and warlock all abroad
Revels keep by field and yard.

In the firelight of the farm
Boy and maiden one by one
Place their chestnuts in the grate
And for omens quietly wait;
To a string their apples tie,
Twirl them till they fallen lie;
Those whose fruits fall in a hurry,
They shall be the first to marry.

Witch and warlock all abroad
Revels keep by field and yard.

Apples from the beams hang down
To be caught by mouth alone,
Mugs of ale on Nut-Crack Night
And many a tale of ghost and sprite,
Come to cheer and chill the heart,
While the candles faint and start,
While the flickering firelight paints
Pictures of the hallowed saints.

Witch and warlock all abroad
Revels keep by field and yard.

Pauline Clarke

A Witch's Song

Now I'm furnished for the flight,
Now I go, now I fly,
Malkin my sweet spirit and I.
O, what a dainty pleasure 'tis
To ride in the air
When the moon shines fair,
And sing and dance and toy and kiss.
Over woods, high rocks and mountains,
Over seas, our mistress' fountains,
Over steeples, towers, and turrets,
We fly by night, 'mongst troops of spirits.

12

No ring of bells to our ears sounds,
No howls of wolves, no yelp of hounds.
No, not the noise of water's breach,
Or cannon's throat can our height reach.

Thomas Middleton

Mother Maudlin the Witch

Within a gloomy dimble she doth dwell
Down in a pit o'ergrown with brakes and briars,
Close by the ruins of a shaken abbey
Torn, with an earthquake, down unto the ground,
'Mongst graves, and grots, near an old charnel house,
Where you shall find her sitting in her form,
As fearful, and melancholic, as that
She is about; with caterpillar's kells,
And knotty cobwebs, rounded in with spells;
Thence she steals forth to relief, in the fogs,
And rotten mists, upon the fens, and bogs,
Down to the drowned lands of Lincolnshire;
To make ewes cast their lambs . . .

Ben Jonson

dimble: ravine or gully
kells: cocoons
relief: seek food

The Hag

The Hag is astride,
   This night for to ride;
The Devil and she together:
   Through thick, and through thin,
   Now out, and then in,
Though ne'er so foul be the weather.

A Thorn or a Burr
   She takes for a Spur:
With a lash of a Bramble she rides now,
   Through Brakes and through Briars,
   O'er Ditches, and Mires,
She follows the Spirit that guides now.

No Beast, for his food,
   Dares now range the wood;
But hush't in his lair he lies lurking:
   While mischiefs, by these,
   On Land and on Seas,
At noon of Night are a-working.

The storm will arise,
   And trouble the skies;
This night, and more for the wonder,
   The ghost from the Tomb
   Affrighted shall come,
Called out by the clap of the Thunder.

Robert Herrick

Hallowe'en

This is the night when witches fly
On their whizzing broomsticks through the wintry sky;
Steering up the pathway where the stars are strewn,
They stretch skinny fingers to the waking moon.

This is the night when old wives tell
Strange and creepy stories, tales of charm and spell;
Peering at the pictures flaming in the fire
They wait for whispers from a ghostly choir.

This is the night when angels go
In and out the houses, winging o'er the snow;
Clearing out the demons from the countryside
They make it new and ready for Christmastide.

Leonard Clark

Look Out, Boys!

Look out! Look out, boys! Clear the track!
The witches are here! They've all come back!
They hanged them high, – No use! No use!
What cares a witch for the hangman's noose?
They buried them deep, but they wouldn't lie still,
For cats and witches are hard to kill;
They swore they shouldn't and wouldn't die, –
Books said they did, but they lie! they lie!

Oliver Wendell Holmes

Witches Gather

Dame, dame! the watch is set:
Quickly come, we all are met.
From the lakes and from the fens,
From the rocks and from the dens,
From the woods and from the caves,
From the churchyards, from the graves,
From the dungeon, from the tree
That they die on, here are we!

The weather is fair, the wind is good:
Up, dame, on your horse of wood!
Or else tuck up your grey frock,
And saddle your goat or your green cock,
And make his bridle a ball of thread
To toll up how many miles you have rid.
Quickly come away,
For we all stay.

The owl is abroad, the bat and the toad,
    And so is the cat-a-mountain;
The ant and the mole sit both in a hole,
    And the frog peeps out of the fountain.
The dogs they do bay, and the timbrels play,
    The spindle is now a-turning;
The moon it is red, and the stars are fled,
    But the sky is a-burning.

                              Ben Jonson

hist   whist
little ghostthings
tip-toe
twinkle-toe

little twitchy
witches and tingling
goblins
hob-a-nob   hob-a-nob

little hoppy happy
toad in tweeds
tweeds
little itchy mousies

with scuttling
eyes   rustle and run   and
hidehidehide
whisk

whisk   look out for the old woman
with the wart on her nose
what she'll do to yer
nobody knows

for she knows the devil   ooch
the devil   ouch
the devil
ach   the great

green
dancing
devil
devil

devil
devil

        wheeEEE

e. e. cummings

The Making of a Charm

First Witch: Round about the cauldron go;
In the poison'd entrails throw.
Toad, that under cold stone
Days and night has thirty-one
Swelter'd venom sleeping got,
Boil thou first i' the charmed pot.

All: Double, double toil and trouble;
Fire, burn; and, caldron, bubble.

Second Witch: Fillet of a fenny snake,
In the cauldron boil and bake;
Eye of newt, and toe of frog,
Wool of bat, and tongue of dog,
Adder's fork, and blind-worm's sting,
Lizard's leg, and howlet's wing, –
For a charm of powerful trouble,
Like a hell-broth boil and bubble.

All: Double, double toil and trouble;
Fire, burn; and, caldron, bubble.

Third Witch: Scale of dragon, tooth of wolf,
Witches' mummy, maw and gulf
Of the ravin'd salt-sea shark,
Root of hemlock digg'd i' the dark,
Liver of blaspheming Jew,
Gall of goat, and slips of yew
Sliver'd in the moon's eclipse,
Nose of Turk, and Tartar's lips,
Finger of birth-strangled babe
Ditch-deliver'd by a drab,
Make the gruel thick and slab:
Add thereto a tiger's chaudron,
For th' ingredients of our cauldron.

All: Double, double toil and trouble;
Fire, burn; and, caldron, bubble.

Second Witch:	Cool it with a baboon's blood,
	Then the charm is firm and good.
	By the pricking of my thumbs,
	Something wicked this way comes:
	Open, locks,
	Whoever knocks!
Macbeth:	How now, you secret, black, and midnight hags!
	What is't you do?
All:	A deed without a name.

William Shakespeare

I Saw Three Witches

I saw three witches
That bowed down like barley,
And took to their brooms 'neath a louring sky,
And, mounting a storm-cloud,
Aloft on its margin,
Stood black in the silver as up they did fly.

I saw three witches
That mocked the poor sparrows
They carried in cages of wicker along,
Till a hawk from his eyrie
Swooped down like an arrow,
And smote on the cages, and ended their song.

I saw three witches
That sailed in a shallop
All turning their heads with a truculent smile
Till a bank of green osiers
Concealed their grim faces,
Though I heard them lamenting for many a mile.

I saw three witches
Asleep in a valley,
Their heads in a row, like stones in a flood,
Till the moon, creeping upward,
Looked white through the valley,
And turned them to bushes in bright scarlet bud.

Walter de la Mare

20

The Witch

I have walked a great while over the snow,
And I am not tall nor strong.
My clothes are wet, and my teeth are set,
And the way was hard and long.
I have wandered over the fruitful earth,
But I never came here before.
Oh, lift me over the threshold, and let me in at the door!

The cutting wind is a cruel foe.
I dare not stand in the blast.
My hands are stone, and my voice a groan,
And the worst of death is past.
I am but a little maiden still,
My little white feet are sore.
Oh, lift me over the threshold, and let me in at the door!

Her voice was the voice that women have,
Who plead for their heart's desire.
She came – she came – and the quivering flame
Sank and died in the fire.
It never was lit again on my hearth
Since I hurried across the floor,
To lift her over the threshold, and let her in at the door.

                                        Mary Coleridge

Hey-How for Hallowe'en!

Hey-How for Hallowe'en!
A' the witches tae be seen,
Some black, an' some green,
Hey-how for Hallowe'en!

                                        Anon

A Country Witch

There's that old hag Moll Brown,
   look, see, just past!
I wish the ugly sly old witch
Would tumble over in the ditch;
I wouldn't pick her out not very fast.
I don't think she's belied, 'tis clear's the sun
That she's a witch if ever there was one.
Yes, I do know just hereabout of two
Or three folks that have learnt
   what Moll can do.
She did, one time, a pretty deal of harm
To Farmer Gruff's folks, down at Lower Farm.
One day, you know,
   they happened to offend her,

And not a little to their sorrow,
Because they would not give or lend her
The thing she came to beg or borrow;
And so, you know, they soon began to find
That she'd a-left her evil wish behind.
She soon bewitched them;
   and she had such power,
That she did make their milk and ale turn sour,
And addle all the eggs their fowls did lay;
They couldn't fetch the butter in the churn,
And cheeses soon began to turn
All back again to curds and whey.
The little pigs a-running with the sow
Did sicken somehow, nobody knew how,
And fall, and turn their snouts towards the sky,
And only give one little grunt and die;
And all the little ducks and chicken
Were death-struck while they were a-pickin'
Their food, and fell upon their head,
And flapped their wings
   and dropped down dead.

They couldn't fat the calves;
  they wouldn't thrive;
They couldn't save their lambs alive;
Their sheep all took the rot and gave no wool;
Their horses fell away to skin and bones,
And got so weak they couldn't pull
A half a peck of stones;
The dog got dead-alive and drowsy,
The cat fell sick and wouldn't mousey;
And if the wretched souls went up to bed
The hag did come and ride them all half dead.
They used to keep her out o' the house 'tis true,
A-nailing up at door a horse's shoe;
And I've a-heard the farmer's wife did try
To drive a needle or a pin
In through her old hard withered skin
And draw her blood, a-coming by;
But she could never fetch a drop,
She bent the pin and broke the needle's top
Against her skin, you know, and that, of course,
Did only make the hag bewitch them worse!

William Barnes

Punkie Night

It's Punkie Night, tonight,
It's Punkie Night, tonight,
Give us a candle, give us a light,
It's Punkie Night tonight.

Anon

Punkie Night: Hallowe'en

Queen Nefertiti

Spin a coin, spin a coin,
    All fall down;
Queen Nefertiti
    Stalks through the town.

Over the pavements
    Her feet go clack,
Her legs are as tall
    As a chimney stack;

Her fingers flicker
    Like snakes in the air,
The walls split open
    At her green-eyed stare;

Her voice is thin
    As the ghosts of bees;
She will crumble your bones,
    She will make your blood freeze.

Spin a coin, spin a coin,
    All fall down;
Queen Nefertiti
    Stalks through the town.

Anon

The Witches' Call

Come, witches, come, on your hithering brooms!
The moorland is dark and still –
Over the church and the churchyard tombs
To the oakwood under the hill.
Come through the mist and wandering cloud,
Fly with the crescent moon;
Come where the witches and warlocks crowd,
Come soon . . . soon!

Leave your room with its shadowy cat,
Your cauldron over the hearth;
Seize your cloak and pointed hat,
Come by the witches' path.
Float from the earth like a rising bird,
Stream through the darkening air,
Come at the sound of our secret word,
Come to the witches' lair!

Clive Sansom

Some Say

Some say the deil's deid,
The deil's deid, the deil's deid,
Some say the deil's deid,
An' buried in Kirkcaldy.

Some say he'll rise again,
Rise again, rise again,
Some say he'll rise again,
An' dance the Hielan Laddie.

Anon

The Two Magicians

O She looked out of the window,
  As white as any milk;
But He looked into the window,
  As black as any silk.

Chorus: Hallo, hallo, hallo, hallo, you coal-black smith!
         O what is your silly song?
         You never shall change my maiden name
         That I have kept so long;
         I'd rather die a maid, yes, but then she said,
         And be buried all in my grave,
         Than I'd have such a nasty, husky, dusky, musty, fusky,
         Coal-black smith.
                        A maiden I will die.

Then She became a duck,
  A duck all on the stream;
And He became a water-dog,
  And fetched her back again.

Chorus: Hallo, hallo, hallo, hallo, you coal-black smith!
         O what is your silly song?
         You never shall change my maiden name
         That I have kept so long;
         I'd rather die a maid, yes, but then she said,
         And be buried all in my grave,
         Than I'd have such a nasty, husky, dusky, musty, fusky,
         Coal-black smith.
                        A maiden I will die.

Then She became a hare,
  A hare all on the plain;
And He became a greyhound dog,
  And fetched her back again.

Chorus: Hallo, hallo, hallo, hallo, you coal-black smith!
         O what is your silly song?
         You never shall change my maiden name
         That I have kept so long;
         I'd rather die a maid, yes, but then she said,
         And be buried all in my grave,
         Than I'd have such a nasty, husky, dusky, musty, fusky,
         Coal-black smith.
                    A maiden I will die.

Then She became a fly,
  A fly all in the air;
And He became a spider,
  And fetched her to his lair.

Chorus: Hallo, hallo, hallo, hallo, you coal-black smith!
         O what is your silly song?
         You never shall change my maiden name
         That I have kept so long;
         I'd rather die a maid, yes, but then she said,
         And be buried all in my grave,
         Than I'd have such a nasty, husky, dusky, musty, fusky,
         Coal-black smith.
                    A maiden I will die.

                              Anon

The Witches' Reel

Cummer go ye before, cummer go ye,
If ye willna go before, cummer let me,
    Ring-a-ring a-widdershins
    Linkin' lithely widdershins
Cummer carlin crone and queen
    Roun' go we!

Cummer go ye before, cummer go ye,
If ye willna go before, cummer let me,
    Ring-a-ring a-widdershins
    Loupin' lightly widdershins
Kilted coats and fleeing hair
    Three times three.

Cummer go ye before, cummer go ye,
If ye willna go before, cummer let me,
    Ring-a-ring a-widdershins
    Whirlin' skirlin' widdershins
And devil take the hindermost
    Who ever she be!

                Anon

A Charm for Travellers

Here I am and forth I must:
In Jesus Christ is all my trust.
No wicked thing do me no spite,
Here nor elsewhere, day nor night.
The Holy Ghost and the Trinity
Come betwixt my evil spirit and me.

                Anon

Strange Visitors

The Strange Visitor

A wife was sitting at her reel ae night;
　And aye she sat, and aye she reeled, and aye she
　　wished for company.

In came a pair o' braid braid soles, and sat down
　　at the fireside;
　And aye she sat, and aye she reeled, and aye she
　　wished for company.

In came a pair o' sma' sma' legs, and sat down on the
　　braid braid soles;
　And aye she sat, and aye she reeled, and aye she
　　wished for company.

In came a pair o' muckle muckle knees, and sat down
　　on the sma' sma' legs;
　And aye she sat, and aye she reeled, and aye she
　　wished for company.

In came a pair o' sma' sma' thees, and sat down on
　　the muckle muckle knees;
　And aye she sat, and aye she reeled, and aye she
　　wished for company.

In came a pair o' muckle muckle hips, and sat down on
　　the sma' sma' thees;
　And aye she sat, and aye she reeled, and aye she
　　wished for company.

In came a sma' sma' waist, and sat down on the
　　muckle muckle hips;
　And aye she sat, and aye she reeled, and aye she
　　wished for company.

In came a pair o' braid braid shouthers, and sat down
　　on the sma' sma' waist;
　And aye she sat, and aye she reeled, and aye she
　　wished for company.

In came a pair o' sma' sma' arms, and sat down on
    the braid braid shouthers;
  And aye she sat, and aye she reeled, and aye she
    wished for company.

In came a pair o' muckle muckle hands, and sat down
    on the sma' sma' arms;
  And aye she sat, and aye she reeled, and aye she
    wished for company.

In came a sma' sma' neck, and sat down on
    the braid braid shouthers;
  And aye she sat, and aye she reeled, and aye she
    wished for company.

In came a great big head, and sat down on
    the sma' sma' neck;
  And aye she sat, and aye she reeled, and aye she
    wished for company.

'What way hae ye sic braid braid feet?' quo' the wife.
'Muckle ganging, muckle ganging.'
'What way hae ye sic sma' sma' legs?'
'*Aih-h-h*! – late – and *wee-e-e* moul.'
'What way hae ye sic muckle muckle knees?'
'Muckle praying, muckle praying.'
'What way hae ye sic sma' sma' thees?'
'*Aih-h-h*! – late – and *wee-e-e* moul.'
'What way hae ye sic big big hips?'
'Muckle sitting, muckle sitting.'
'What way hae ye sic a sma' sma' waist?'
'*Aih-h-h*! – late – and *wee-e-e* moul.'
'What way hae ye sic braid braid shouthers?'
'Wi' carrying broom, wi' carrying broom.'
'What way hae ye sic sma' sma' arms?'
'*Aih-h-h*! – late – and *wee-e-e* moul.'
'What way hae ye sic muckle muckle hands?'
'Threshing wi' an iron flail, threshing wi' an iron flail.'
'What way hae ye sic a sma' sma' neck?'
'*Aih-h-h*! – late – and *wee-e-e* moul.'
'What way hae ye sic a muckle muckle head?'

'Muckle wit, muckle wit.'
'What do you come for?'
'For YOU!'

Anon

reel : a frame for winding yarn   *thees : thighs*
ae : one   *shouthers : shoulders*
braid : broad   *sic : such*
muckle : big   *muckle ganging : much walking*

Unwelcome

We were young, we were merry, we were very very wise,
  And the door stood open at our feast,
When there passed us a woman with the West in her eyes,
  And a man with his back to the East.

O, still grew the hearts that were beating so fast,
  The loudest voice was still.
The jest died away on our lips as they passed,
  And the rays of July struck chill.

The cups of red wine turned pale on the board,
  The white bread black as soot.
The hound forgot the hand of her lord,
  She fell down at his foot.

Low let me lie, where the dead dog lies,
  Ere I sit me down again at a feast,
When there passes a woman with the West in her eyes,
  And a man with his back to the East.

Mary Coleridge

Oft in the Lone Churchyard

Oft in the lone churchyard at night I've seen,
By glimpse of moon-shine chequering through the trees,
The school-boy with his satchel in his hand,
Whistling aloud to bear his courage up,
And lightly tripping o'er the long flat stones,
(With nettles skirted, and with moss o'ergrown),
That tell in homely phrase who lie below.
Sudden he starts, and hears, or thinks he hears,
The sound of something purring at his heels;
Full fast he flies, and dares not look behind him,
Till out of breath he overtakes his fellows;
Who gather round, and wonder at the tale
Of horrid apparition, tall and ghastly,
That walks at dead of night, or takes his stand
O'er some new-open'd grave; and (strange to tell!)
Vanishes at crowing of the cock.

Robert Blair

Sweet William's Ghost

There came a ghost to Margret's door,
   With many a grievous groan,
And for long he pulled at the pin
   But answer made she none.

'Is it my father Philip?
   Or is't my brother John?
Or is't my true love Willie
   From Scotland new come home?'

' 'Tis not thy father Philip,
    Nor yet thy brother John,
But 'tis thy true love Willie,
    From Scotland new come home.

'O sweet Margret! O dear Margret!
    I pray thee speak to me;
Give me my faith and troth, Margret,
    As I give it to thee.'

'Thy faith and troth thou'lt never get,
    Of me shalt never win,
Till that thou come within my bower
    And kiss me cheek and chin.'

'If I should come within thy bower,
    I am no earthly man;
And should I kiss thy rosy lips,
    Thy days would not be long.

'O sweet Margret! O dear Margret!
    I pray thee speak to me;
Give me my faith and troth, Margret,
    As I gave them to thee.'

'Thy faith and troth thou'lt never get,
    Of me shalt never win,
Till that thou take me to yon kirkyard
    And wed me with a ring.'

'My bones are in a kirkyard laid
    Afar beyond the sea;
And it is but my ghost, Margret,
    That speaketh now to thee.'

She stretched out her lily hand,
    As for to do her best,
'Have there your faith and troth, Willie,
    God send your soul good rest!'

She kilted up her robes of green,
    A piece below her knee;
And all the live-long winter night
    The dead corpse followed she.

'Is there any room at your head, Willie,
    Is there any room at your feet,
Is there any room at your side, Willie,
    Wherein I might creep?'

'There's no room at my head, Margret,
    There's no room at my feet,
There's no room at my side, Margret,
    My coffin is made so meet.'

Then up and crew the red, red cock,
    And up and crew the grey;
' 'Tis time, 'tis time, my dear Margret,
    That I was gone away.'

No more the ghost to Margret said
    But with a grievous moan
Vanished in a cloud of mist,
    And left her all alone.

'O stay, my only true-love, stay',
    The constant Margret cried;
Wan grew her cheeks, she closed her eyes,
    Stretched her soft limbs, and died.

                              Anon

Prayer for a Quiet Night

Let no lamenting cries, nor doleful tears
Be heard all night within, nor yet without:
Nor let false whispers, breeding hidden fears,
Break gentle sleep with misconceived doubt.
Let no deluding dreams, nor dreadful sights,
Make sudden sad affrights;
Nor let house-fires, nor lightning's helpless harms
Nor let the Puck, nor other evil sprights,
Nor let mischievous witches with their charms,
Nor let hobgoblins, names whose sense we see not,
Fray us with things that be not:
Let not the screech owl nor the stork be heard,
Nor the night raven that still deadly yells:
Nor damned ghosts, called up with mighty spells,
Nor grisly vultures, make us once affeared:
Nor let unpleasant choir of frogs still croaking
Make us to wish their choking.
Let none of these their dreary accents sing:
Nor let the woods them answer, nor their echoes ring.

Edmund Spenser

Charm for the Coming Day

In the morning when ye rise
Wash your hands, and cleanse your eyes.
Next be sure ye have a care,
To disperse the water farre.
For as farre as that doth light,
So farre keepes the evill Spright.

Robert Herrick

Cold Lies the Dew

There was an old Granny who lost her sight,
Cold lies the Dew.
She couldn't tell if it were morning or night,
Cold lies the Dew.
There come a fine gentleman, black as a coal,
'I'll give 'ee some eyes, if you'll sell me your soul,'
Cold lies the Dew.

She gave him a criss-cross, she muttered a prayer,
Cold lies the Dew.
And off with a scritch he went up in the air,
Cold lies the Dew.
The poor old Granny she longed for her eyes,
And down on her knees goes her head and she cries,
Cold lies the Dew.

There came a pit-patter and Somebody says,
Cold lies the Dew,
'All your long life you've a-minded our ways,
Cold lies the Dew,
With pail of spring water and cream bowl too'
They led her away in the May morning dew,
Cold lies the Dew.

Her sight came back, it was clear and fine,
Cold lies the Dew.
Her pretty blue eyes they was all a-shine,
Cold lies the Dew.
She stood all alone there – Then who were 'They'?
The wise old Granny she never would say,
Cold lies the Dew.

Anon

Prince Kano

In a dark wood Prince Kano lost his way
And searched in vain through the long summer's day.
At last, when night was near, he came in sight
Of a small clearing filled with yellow light,
And there, bending beside his brazier, stood
A charcoal burner wearing a black hood.
The Prince cried out for joy: 'Good friend, I'll give
What you will ask: guide me to where I live.'
The man pulled back his hood: he had no face –
Where it should be there was an empty space.

Half dead with fear the Prince staggered away,
Rushed blindly through the wood till break of day;
And then he saw a larger clearing, filled
With houses, people; but his soul was chilled,
He looked around for comfort, and his search
Led him inside a small, half-empty church
Where monks prayed. 'Father,' to one he said,
'I've seen a dreadful thing; I am afraid.'
'What did you see, my son?' 'I saw a man
Whose face was like . . .' and, as the Prince began,
The monk drew back his hood and seemed to hiss,
Pointing to where his face should be, 'Like this?'

Edward Lowbury

Charm against Witches

Bring the holy crust of Bread,
Lay it underneath the head;
'Tis a certain Charme to keep
Hags away, while Children sleep.

Robert Herrick

Daniel Webster's Horses

If when the wind blows
Rattling the trees
Clicking like skeletons'
Elbows and knees,

You hear along the road
Three horses pass –
Do not go near the dark
Cold window glass.

If when the first snow lies
Whiter than bones
You see the mark of hoofs
Cut to the stones,

Hoofs of three horses
Going abreast –
Turn about, turn about,
A closed door is best!

Upright in the earth
Under the sod
They buried three horses
Bridled and shod,

Daniel Webster's horses –
He said as he grew old,
"Flesh, I loved riding,
Shall I not love it, cold?

"Shall I not love to ride
Bone astride bone,
When the cold wind blows
And snow covers stone?

"Bury them on their feet
With bridle and bit.
They were fine horses –
See their shoes fit."

Elizabeth Coatsworth

Shadow-Bride

There was a man who dwelt alone,
   as day and night went past.
He sat as still as carven stone,
   and yet no shadow cast.
The white owls perched upon his head
   beneath the winter moon;
they wiped their beaks and thought him dead
   under the stars of June.

There came a lady clad in grey
   in the twilight shining;
one moment she would stand and stay,
   her hair with flowers entwining.
He woke, as had he sprung of stone,
   and broke the spell that bound him;
he clasped her fast, both flesh and bone,
   and wrapped her shadow round him.

There never more she walks her ways
   by sun or moon or star;
she dwells below where neither days
   nor any nights there are.
But once a year when caverns yawn
   and hidden things awake,
they dance together then till dawn
   and a single shadow make.

J. R. R. Tolkien

The Spunky

The Spunky he went like a sad little flame,
All, all alone.
All out on the zogs and a-down the lane,
All, all alone.
A tinker came by that was full of ale,
And into the mud he went head over tail,
All, all alone.

A crotchety Farmer came riding by,
All, all alone.
He cursed him low and he cursed him high,
All, all alone.
The Spunky he up and he led him astray,
The pony were foundered until it were day,
All, all alone.

There came an old Granny – she see the small Ghost,
All, all alone.
'Yew poor liddle soul all a-cold, a-lost,
All, all alone.
I'll give 'ee a criss-cross to save 'ee bide;
Be off to the Church and make merry inside,
All, all alone.'

The Spunky he laughed, 'Here I'll galley no more!'
All, all alone.
And off he did wiver and in at the door,
All, all alone.
The souls they did sing for to end his pain,
There's no little Spunky a-down the lane,
All, all alone.

Anon

Restless Spirits

Will-O'-Wisp

I've seen the midnight morris-dance of hell
On the black moors while thicker darkness fell,
Like dancing lamps or bounding balls of fire,
Now in and out, now up and down, now higher,
As though an unseen horseman in his flight
Flew swinging up and down a lamp alight;
Then fixed, as though it feared its end to meet,
It shone as lamps shine in a stilly street;
Then all at once it shot and danced anew,
Till mixed with darkness out of sight it grew.
The simple shepherd under fear's eclipse
Views the dread omens of these will-o'-wisps,
And thinks them haunting spirits of the earth
That shine where midnight murders had their birth;
With souls of midnight and with heads of fire
To him they shine, and bound o'er moor and mire,
Blazing like burning, crackling wisps of straw;
He sees and hears them, then with sudden awe
He pictures thieves with lanthorn light in hand,
That in lone spots for murder waiting stand.
Upon the meadow bridge's very wall
He sees a lanthorn stand, and pictures all
The muttered voices that derange his ears;
And when more near the spot, his sickening fears
See the imagined lanthorn, light and all,
Without a plash into the water fall,
And in one moment on his stifled sight
It blanks his hopes and sets his terrors right.
For furlongs off it simmers up and down,
A will-o'-wisp; and breathless to the town

He hastes, and hardly dares to catch his breath,
Existing like a doubt of life or death
Until the sight of houses cools his fears
And fireside voices greet his happy ears.
And then he rubs his hands beside the fire,
And quakes, and tells how over moor and mire
The jack-o'-lanthorn with his burning tails
Had like to lead him.

John Clare

A Charm

Thrice toss these oaken ashes in the air;
Thrice sit thou mute in this enchanted chair;
Then thrice three times tie up this true love's knot,
And murmur soft: 'She will, or she will not.'

Go burn these poisonous weeds in yon blue fire,
These screech-owl's feathers and this prickling briar,
This cypress gathered at a dead man's grave,
That all thy fears and cares an end may have;

Then come, you fairies, dance with me a round;
Melt her hard heart with your melodious sound.
In vain are all the charms I can devise;
She hath an art to break them with her eyes.

Thomas Campion

Bewitched

I have heard a lady this night,
　Lissom and jimp and slim,
Calling me – calling me over the heather,
　'Neath the beech boughs dusk and dim.

I have followed a lady this night,
　Followed her far and lone,
Fox and adder and weasel know
　The ways that we have gone.

I sit at my supper 'mid honest faces,
　And crumble my crust and say
Naught in the long-drawn drawl of the voices
　Talking the hours away.

I'll go to my chamber under the gable,
　And the moon will lift her light
In at my lattice from over the moorland
　Hollow and still and bright.

And I know she will shine on a lady of witchcraft,
　Gladness and grief to see,
Who has taken my heart with her nimble fingers,
　Calls in my dreams to me;

Who has led me a dance by dell and dingle
　My human soul to win,
Made me a changeling to my own, own mother,
　A stranger to my kin.

　　　　　　　　Walter de la Mare

The Changeling

Toll no bell for me, dear Father, dear Mother,
    Waste no sighs;
There are my sisters, there is my little brother
    Who plays in the place called Paradise,
Your children all, your children for ever;
    But I, so wild,
Your disgrace, with the queer brown face, was never,
    Never, I know, but half your child!

In the garden at play, all day, last summer,
    Far and away I heard
The sweet "tweet-tweet" of a strange new-comer,
    The dearest, clearest call of a bird.
It lived down there in the deep green hollow,
    My own old home, and the fairies say
The word of a bird is a thing to follow,
    So I was away a night and a day.

One evening, too, by the nursery fire,
    We snuggled close and sat round so still,
When suddenly as the wind blew higher,
    Something scratched on the window-sill,
A pinched brown face peered in – I shivered;
    No one listened or seemed to see;
The arms of it waved and the wings of it quivered,
    Whoo – I knew it had come for me!
    Some are as bad as bad can be!

All night long they danced in the rain,
Round and round in a dripping chain,
Threw their caps at the window-pane,
    Tried to make me scream and shout
    And fling the bedclothes all about:
I meant to stay in bed that night,
And if only you had left a light
    They would never have got me out!

Sometimes I wouldn't speak, you see,
Or answer when you spoke to me,
Because in the long, still dusks of Spring
You can hear the whole world whispering;
   The shy green grasses making love,
   The feathers grow on the dear grey dove,
   The tiny heart of the redstart beat,
   The patter of the squirrel's feet,
The pebbles pushing in the silver streams,
The rushes talking in their dreams,
   The swish-swish of the bat's black wings,
   The wild-wood bluebell's sweet ting-tings,
     Humming and hammering at your ear,
     Everything there is to hear
In the heart of hidden things.
   But not in the midst of the nursery riot,
   That's why I wanted to be quiet,
     Couldn't do my sums, or sing,
     Or settle down to anything.
   And when, for that, I was sent upstairs
   I *did* kneel down to say my prayers;
But the King who sits on your high church steeple
Has nothing to do with us fairy people!

'Times I pleased you, dear Father, dear Mother,
   Learned all my lessons and liked to play,
And dearly I loved the little pale brother
   Whom some other bird must have called away.
Why did they bring me here to make me
   Not quite bad and not quite good,
Why, unless They're wicked, do They want, in spite, to take me
     Back to Their wet, wild wood?
Now, every night I shall see the windows shining,
   The gold lamp's glow, and the fire's red gleam,
While the best of us are twining twigs and the rest of us are whining
     In the hollow by the stream.

Black and chill are Their nights on the wold;
   And They live so long and They feel no pain:
I shall grow up, but never grow old,
I shall always, always be very cold,
      I shall never come back again!

Charlotte Mew

Traveller's Curse After Misdirection

(From the Welsh)

May they stumble, stage by stage
On an endless pilgrimage,
Dawn and dusk, mile after mile,
At each and every step, a stile;
At each and every step withal
May they catch their feet and fall;
At each and every fall they take
May a bone within them break:
And may the bone that breaks within
Not be, for variation's sake,
Now rib, now thigh, now arm, now shin,
But always, without fail, THE NECK.

Robert Graves

The Little Boy Lost

The wood was rather old and dark
The witch was very ugly
And if it hadn't been for father
Walking there so smugly
I never should have followed
The beckoning of her finger.
Ah me how long ago it was
And still I linger
Under the ever interlacing beeches
Over a carpet of moss.
I lift my hand but it never reaches
To where the breezes toss
The sun-kissed leaves above.
The sun?
Beware.
The sun never comes here.
Round about and round I go
Up and down and to and fro,
The woodlouse hops upon the tree
Or should do but I really cannot see.
Happy fellow. Why can't I be
Happy as he?
The wood grows darker every day
It's now a bad place in a way
But I lost the way
Last Tuesday.
Did I love father, mother, home?
Not very much; but now they're gone
I think of them with kindly toleration
Bred inevitably of separation.
Really if I could find some food
I should be happy enough in this wood
But darker days and hungrier I must spend
Till hunger and darkness make an end.

Stevie Smith

A Spell for Sleeping

Sweet william, silverweed, sally-my-handsome.
Dimity darkens the pittering water.
On gloomed lawns wanders a king's daughter.

Curtains are clouding the casement windows.
A moon-glade smurrs the lake with light.
Doves cover the tower with quiet.

Three owls whit-whit in the withies.
Seven fish in a deep pool shimmer.
The princess moves to the spiral stair.

Slowly the sickle moon mounts up.
Frogs hump under moss and mushroom.
The princess climbs to her high hushed room,

Step by step to her shadowed tower.
Water laps the white lake shore.
A ghost opens the princess's door.

Seven fish in the sway of the water.
Six candles for a king's daughter.
Five sighs for a drooping head.
Four ghosts to gentle her bed.
Three owls in the dusk falling.
Two tales to be telling.
One spell for sleeping.

Tamarisk, trefoil, tormentil.
Sleep rolls down from the clouded hill.
A princess dreams of a silver pool.

The moonlight spreads, the soft ferns flitter.
Stilled in a shimmering drift of water,
Seven fish dream of a lost king's daughter.

Alastair Reid

The Song of Wandering Aengus

I went out to the hazel wood,
Because a fire was in my head,
And cut and peeled a hazel wand
And hooked a berry to a thread;
And when white moths were on the wing,
And moth-like stars were flickering out,
I dropped· the berry in a stream
And caught a little silver trout.

When I had laid it on the floor
I went to blow the fire aflame,
But something rustled on the floor
And someone called me by my name:
It had become a glimmering girl
With apple blossom in her hair
Who called me by my name and ran
And faded through the brightening air.

Though I am old with wandering
Through hollow lands and hilly lands
I will find out where she has gone,
And kiss her lips and take her hands;
And walk among long dappled grass,
And pluck till time and times are done
The silver apples of the moon,
The golden apples of the sun.

                    W. B. Yeats

La Belle Dame Sans Merci

"O what can ail thee, knight-at-arms,
Alone and palely loitering?
The sedge has withered from the lake,
   And no birds sing.

"O what can ail thee, knight-at-arms,
   So haggard and so woe-begone?
The squirrel's granary is full,
   And the harvest's done.

"I see a lily on thy brow
   With anguish moist and fever dew,
And on thy cheek a fading rose
   Fast withereth too."

I met a lady in the meads,
   Full beautiful – a faery's child,
Her hair was long, her foot was light,
   And her eyes were wild.

I made a garland for her head,
   And bracelets too, and fragrant zone,
She looked at me as she did love,
   And made sweet moan.

I set her on my pacing steed,
   And nothing else saw all day long,
For sidelong would she bend, and sing
   A faery's song.

She found me roots of relish sweet,
   And honey wild, and manna dew,
And sure in language strange she said –
   "I love thee true!"

She took me to her elfin grot,
   And there she wept and sighed full sore,
And there I shut her wild, wild eyes
   With kisses four.

And there she lulled me asleep,
   And there I dreamed – ah! woe betide!
The latest dream I ever dreamed
   On the cold hill's side.

I saw pale kings and princes too,
   Pale warriors, death-pale were they all;
They cried – "La Belle Dame sans Merci
   Hath thee in thrall!"

I saw their starved lips in the gloam,
   With horrid warning gaped wide,
And I awoke and found me here,
   On the cold hill's side.

And this is why I sojourn here,
   Alone and palely loitering,
Though the sedge is withered from the lake,
   And no birds sing.

                John Keats

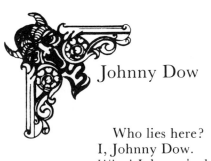

Johnny Dow

    Who lies here?
I, Johnny Dow.
Who! Johnny is that you?
Aye, man, but I'm dead now.

                Anon

The Demon Lover

'O where have you been, my long-lost love,
    These long seven years and more?'
'O I'm come to seek my former vows,
    That you promised me before.'

'O hold your tongue of your former vows,
    For they'll breed bitter strife,
O hold your tongue of your former vows,
    For I am become a wife.'

He turned him right and round about,
    And the tear blinded his e'e:
'I would never have trodden on Irish ground
    If it had not been for thee.

'I might have had a noble lady,
    Far, far beyond the sea,
I might have had a noble lady,
    Were it not for the love of thee.'

'If you might have had a noble lady,
    Yourself you have to blame;
You should have taken the noble lady,
    For you knew that I was none.'

'O false are the vows of womenkind,
    But fair is their false body:
I would never have trodden on Irish ground,
    Were it not for the love of thee.'

'O what have you to take me to,
    If I with you should go,
If I were to leave my good husband,
    My little young son also?'

'I have seven ships upon the sea,
   The eighth brought me to land,
With mariners and merchandise,
   And music on every hand.

'The ship wherein my love shall sail,
   Is glorious to behold,
The sails are of the finest silk,
   And the masts of beaten gold.'

She's taken up her little young son,
   Kissed him both cheek and chin.
'O fare you well, my little young son,
   For I'll ne'er see you again!'

They had not sailed a league, a league,
   A league but barely one,
Till she minded on her good husband,
   And on her little young son.

'O if I were at home again,
   At home where I would be,
No living man should flatter me,
   To sail upon the sea!'

'O hold your tongue of weeping,' he says,
   'Let all your follies a-be;
I'll show you where the lilies grow
   On the banks of Italy.'

They had not sailed a league, a league,
   A league but barely three,
Till grim, grim grew his countenance,
   And gurly grew the sea.

'O what hills are you, yon pleasant hills,
    That the sun shines sweetly on?'
'O yon are the hills of Heaven,' he says,
    'Where you will never win.'

'And O what mountain is yon?' she said,
    'So dreary with frost and snow?'
'Yon is the mountain of Hell,' he said,
    'Where you and I must go.

'But hold your tongue, my dearest dear,
    Let all your follies a-be;
I'll show you where the lilies grow
    At the bottom of the sea.'

And aye as she turned her round about,
    Aye taller he seemed to be,
Until the tops of that gallant ship
    No taller were than he.

He struck the top-mast with his hand,
    The fore-mast with his knee:
And he broke that gallant ship in twain,
    And sank her in the sea.

                                Anon

Bewitched

Haunted

Black hill
black hall
all still
owl's grey·cry
edges shrill
castle night.

Woken eye
round in fright;
what lurks walks
in castle rustle?

Hand cold
held hand
the moving roving
urging thing;
dreamed margin

voiceless
noiseless
HEARD
feared
a ghost passed

black hill
black hall
all still
owl's grey cry
edges shrill
castle night.

   William Mayne

The Empty House

Where the lone wind on the hilltop
Shakes the thistles as it passes,
Stirs the quiet-ticking grasses
That keep time outside the door,
Stands a house that's grey and silent;
No one lives there any more.

Wending through the broken .windows,
Every season and its weather
Whisper in those rooms together:
Summer's warm and wandering rains
Rot the leaves of last year's autumn,
Warp the floors that winter stains.

In a papered hall a clock-shape,
Dim and pale on yellowed flowers,
Still remains where rang the hours
Of a clock that's lost and gone.
And the fading ghost keeps no-time
On the wall it lived upon.

On a stairway where no footsteps
Stir the dusty sunlight burning
Sit the patient shadow turning
Speechless faces to the wall
While they hear the silent striking
Of that no-clock in the hall.

"Dawn of no-time! Noon of no-time!"
Cries the phantom echo chiming,
And the shadows, moving, miming,
Slowly shift before the light.
But no eye has seen their motion
When the clock says, "No-time night!"

No eye has seen them dancing
In their blackness fell and bright,
To a silent tune
In the dark of the moon
When the clock sings no-time night.

Russell Hoban

Green Candles

"There's someone at the door," said gold candlestick:
"Let her in quick, let her in quick!"
"There is a small hand groping at the handle.
Why don't you turn it?" asked green candle.

"Don't go, don't go," said the Hepplewhite chair,
"Lest you find a strange lady there."
"Yes, stay where you are," whispered the white wall:
"There is nobody there at all."

"I know her little foot," grey carpet said:
"Who but I should know her light tread?"
"She shall come in," answered the open door,
"And not," said the room, "go out any more."

Humbert Wolfe

The *Alice Jean*

One moonlight night a ship drove in,
   A ghost ship from the west,
Drifting with bare mast and lone tiller;
   Like a mermaid drest
In long green weed and barnacles
   She beached and came to rest.

All the watchers of the coast
   Flocked to view the sight;
Men and women, streaming down
   Through the summer night,
Found her standing tall and ragged
   Beached in the moonlight.

Then one old woman stared aghast:
   "The *Alice Jean?* But no!
The ship that took my Ned from me
   Sixty years ago –
Drifted back from the utmost west
   With the ocean's flow?

"Caught and caged in the weedy pool
   Beyond the western brink,
Where crewless vessels lie and rot
   In waters black as ink,
Torn out at last by a sudden gale –
   Is it the *Jean*, you think?"

A hundred women gaped at her,
   The menfolk nudged and laughed,
But none could find a likelier story
   For the strange craft
With fear and death and desolation
   Rigged fore and aft.

The blind ship came forgotten home
   To all but one of these,
Of whom none dared to climb aboard her:
   And by and by the breeze
Veered hard about, and the *Alice Jean*
   Foundered in foaming seas.

                     Robert Graves

Emperors of the Island

There is the story of a deserted island
where five men walked down to the bay.

The story of the island is
that three men would two men slay.

Three men dug two graves in the sand,
three men stood on the sea wet rock,
three shadows moved away.

There is the story of a deserted island
where three men walked down to the bay.

The story of this island is
that two men would one man slay.

Two men dug one grave in the sand,
two men stood on the sea wet rock,
two shadows moved away.

There is the story of a deserted island
where two men walked down to the bay.

The story of this island is
that one man would one man slay.

One man dug one grave in the sand,
one man stood on the sea wet rock,
one shadow moved away.

There is the story of a deserted island
where four ghosts walked down to the bay.

The story of this island is
that four ghosts would one man slay.

Four ghosts dug one grave in the sand,
four ghosts stood on the sea wet rock;
five ghosts moved away.

Dannie Abse

A Man of Words

A man of words and not of deeds
Is like a garden full of weeds.
When the weeds begin to grow,
It's like a garden full of snow;
When the snow begins to fall,
It's like a bird upon the wall;
When the bird begins to fly,
It's like an eagle in the sky;
When the sky begins to roar,
It's like a lion at the door;
When the door begins to crack,
It's like a whip across your back;
When your back begins to smart,
It's like a penknife in your heart;
And when your heart begins to bleed,
You're dead, you're dead, you're dead indeed.

Anon

The Way Through The Woods

They shut the road through the woods
Seventy years ago.
Weather and rain have undone it again,
And now you would never know
There was once a road through the woods
Before they planted the trees.
It is underneath the coppice and heath,
And the thin anemones.
Only the keeper sees
That, where the ring-dove broods,
And the badgers roll at ease,
There was once a road through the woods.

Yet, if you enter the woods
Of a summer evening late,
When the night-air cools on the trout-ringed pools
Where the otter whistles his mate,
(They fear not men in the woods,
Because they see so few.)
You will hear the beat of a horse's feet,
And the swish of a skirt in the dew,
Steadily cantering through
The misty solitudes,
As though they perfectly knew
The old lost road through the woods . . .
But there is no road through the woods.

Rudyard Kipling

The Ghosts' Walk

They came with lorries, they came with vans, they came in the
    early May;
Room by room and stair by stair they carried the house away;
There was never a brick and never a stone to show where the old
    home stood,
And a couple of family ghosts were left who took to a nearby wood.

The Northern Spring was a genial Spring, and the summer nights
    were fair,
And the two ghosts walked in the gibbous moon and danced
    in the open air.
Autumn came and they weren't so pleased, for the wind waxed
. cold and keen.
And one of the two had a ghostly liver and one had a phantom spleen.

One ghost said to the other ghost, "Alas for the brave old days,
When the walls were strong in the old house and the fires had a
    cheerful blaze."
And the second ghost answered tartly, "That's a fatheaded way to talk,
When there isn't as much as a cupboard left where an indoor ghost
    could walk."

The rain dripped down from the naked boughs, the wind swept in
    through the holes,
Their spinal columns were stiff and damp, and the first said,
    "Blast their souls;
A Tudor house in its early state might well have been left intact."
And the other sat on his hands and said, "It wasn't and that's a fact.

"We might have got in the last sad van and gone where the old
    house went;
We knew they were sticking it up afresh in Surrey or Hants or Kent,
I'm not sure which; but stair by stair and room by room it stands
Where I'd be now if it wasn't for you." And again he sat on his hands.

But mildly the first ghost answered, "For centuries close on nine,
Here we have been with our sons and sires, an honoured and ancient
    line;
Think of the sentiment, Sniffey." The second in charnel tones
Said, "Sentiment's all very well in its place, but sentiment won't
    warm bones."

And the wind swept in through the naked boles, and the rain
    dripped down from the bough,
And the two ghosts huddled together – it was far too cold for a row –
Till the strong ghost said, "Here, up you!"; and, or ever that
    storm was spent,
They were off on a trek from the cheerless North to Surrey – or Hants
    – or Kent.

There's a fearsome story of two pale ghosts that the horrified
    rustic meets
Stalking along by the Great North Road through the villages'
    quiet streets;
Night by night one can mark their trail; we learn from the last report
They've crossed the Thames by Wallingford Bridge, but were going a
    trifle short.

John Kendall

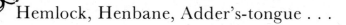

Hemlock, Henbane, Adder's-tongue . . .

I have been all day looking after
A raven feeding upon a quarter;
And, soon as she turn'd her beak to the south,
I snatch'd this morsel out of her mouth.

I last night lay all alone
O' the ground, to hear the mandrake groan;
And pluck'd him up, though he grew full low:
And, as I had done, the cock did crow.

Under a cradle I did creep
By day; and when the child was asleep
At night, I suck'd the breath; and rose,
And pluck'd the nodding nurse by the nose.

A murderer, yonder, was hung in chains;
The sun and the wind had shrunk his veins:
I bit off a sinew; I clipp'd his hair;
I brought off his rags, that danc'd i' the air.

And I ha' been plucking (plants among)
Hemlock, henbane, adder's tongue,
Night-shade, moon-wort, libbard's-bane;
And twice by the dogs was like to be ta'en.

I went to the toad, breeds under the wall,
I charmed him out, and he came at my call;
I scratch'd out the eyes of the owl before;
I tore the bat's wing: what, would you have more?

Yes: I have brought to help your vows,
Horned poppy, cypress boughs,
The fig-tree wild, that grows on tombs,
And juice, that from the larch-tree comes,
    The basilisk's blood, and the viper's skin:
    And now our orgies let's begin.

Ben Jonson

70

Odd Bods

Queer Things

"Very, very queer things have been happening to me
   In some of the places where I've been.
I went to the pillar-box this morning with a letter
   And a hand came out and took it in.

"When I got home again, I thought I'd have
   A glass of spirits to steady myself;
And I take my bible oath, but that bottle and glass
   Came a-hopping down off the shelf.

"No, no, I says, I'd better take no spirits,
   And I sat down to have a cup of tea;
And blowed if my old pair of carpet-slippers
   Didn't walk across the carpet to me!

"So I took my newspaper and went into the park,
   And looked round to see no one was near,
When a voice right out of the middle of the paper
   Started reading the news bold and clear!

"Well, I guess there's some magician out to help me,
   So perhaps there's no need for alarm;
And if I manage not to anger him,
   Why should he do me any harm?"

James Reeves

Mixed Brews

There once was a witch
Who lived in a ditch
And brewed her brews in the hedges.
She gathered some dank
From the deepest bank
And some from around the edges.

She practised her charms
By waving her arms
And muttering words and curses;
And every spell
Would have worked out well
If she hadn't mixed the verses.

Not long since,
When she wanted a Prince
To wake the Sleeping Beauty,
A man appeared
With a long grey beard,
Too old to report for duty!

When she hoped to save
Aladdin's cave
From his uncle cruel and cranky,
She concocted a spell
That somehow fell
Not on him but on Widow Twankey.

With a magic bean
She called for a Queen
Who was locked in the wizard's castle.
There came an old hag
With a postman's bag
And threepence to pay on the parcel.

What *comes* of a witch
Who has hitch after hitch?
I'm afraid that there's no telling:
But I think, as a rule,
She returns to school
And tries to improve her spelling.

Clive Sansom

Old Moll

The moon is up,
  The night owls scritch.
Who's that croaking?
  The frog in the ditch.
Who's that howling?
  The old hound bitch.
My neck tingles,
  My elbows itch,
My hair rises,
  My eyelids twitch.
What's in that pot
  So rare and rich?
Who's that crouching
  In a cloak like pitch?
Hush! that's Old Moll –
  They say she's a
Most ree-markable old party.

James Reeves

Oo-oo-ah-ah!

A woman in a churchyard sat,
   Oo-oo-ah-ah!
Very short and very fat,
   Oo-oo-ah-ah!
She saw three corpses carried in,
   Oo-oo-ah-ah!
Very tall and very thin,
   Oo-oo-ah-ah!

Woman to the corpses said,
   Oo-oo-ah-ah!
Shall I be like you when I am dead?
   Oo-oo-ah-ah!

Corpses to the woman said,
   Oo-oo-ah-ah!
Yes, you'll be like us when you are dead,
   Oo-oo-ah-ah!
Woman to the corpses said –
             (Silence)

         Anon

Two Charms to Cure Hiccups

Hiccup, hiccup, go away,
Come again another day:
Hiccup, hiccup, when I bake,
I'll give to you a butter-cake.

  Hiccup, snickup,
   Rise up, right up,
    Three drops in a cup
Are good for the hiccup.

       Anon

Dinky

O what's the weather in a Beard?
It's windy there, and rather weird,
And when you think the sky has cleared
    – Why, there is Dirty Dinky.

Suppose you walk out in a Storm,
With nothing on to keep you warm,
And then step barefoot on a Worm
    – Of course, it's Dirty Dinky.

As I was crossing a hot hot Plain,
I saw a sight that caused me pain,
You asked me before, I'll tell you again:
    – It *looked* like Dirty Dinky.

Last night you lay a-sleeping? No!
The room was thirty-five below;
The sheets and blankets turned to snow.
    – He'd got in: Dirty Dinky.

You'd better watch the things you do,
You'd better watch the things you do.
You're part of him; he's part of you
    – *You* may be Dirty Dinky.

Theodore Roethke

The Two Witches

O, sixteen hundred and ninety one,
Never was year so well begun,
Backsy-forsy and inside out,
The best of all years to ballad about.

On the first fine day of January
I ran to my sweetheart Margery
And tossed her over the roof so far
That down she fell like a shooting star.

But when we two had frolicked and kissed
She clapped her fingers about my wrist
And tossed me over the chimney stack,
And danced on me till my bones did crack.

Then, when she had laboured to ease my pain,
We sat by the stile of Robin's Lane,
She in a hare and I in a toad
And puffed at the clouds till merry they glowed.

We spelled our loves until close of day.
I wished her goodnight and walked away.
But she put out a tongue that was long and red
And swallowed me down like a crumb of bread.

Robert Graves

A Cure for Cramp

The devil is tying a knot in my leg,
Matthew, Mark, Luke and John, unloose it I beg:
Crosses three we make to ease us,
Two for the thieves and one for Christ Jesus.

Anon

Song of the Ogres

Little fellow, you're amusing,
Stop before you end by losing
  Your shirt:
Run along to Mother, Gus,
Those who interfere with us
  Get hurt.

Honest Virtue, old wives prattle,
Always wins the final battle.
  Dear, Dear!
Life's exactly what it looks,
Love may triumph in the books,
  Not here.

We're not joking, we assure you:
Those who rode this way before you
  Died hard.
What? Still spoiling for a fight?
Well, you've asked for it all right:
  On guard!

Always hopeful, aren't you? Don't be.
Night is falling and it won't be
  Long now:
You will never see the dawn,
You will wish you'd not been born.
  And how!

                    W. H. Auden

The Witch

Weary went the old Witch,
Weary of her pack,
She sat her down by the churchyard wall,
And jerked it off her back.

The cord brake, yes, the cord brake,
Just where the dead did lie,
And Charms and Spells and Sorceries
Spilled out beneath the sky.

Weary was the old Witch;
She rested her old eyes
From the lantern-fruited yew trees,
And the scarlet of the skies;

And out the dead came stumbling,
From every rift and crack,
Silent as moss, and plundered
The gaping pack.

They wish them, three times over,
Away they skip full soon:
Bat and Mole and Leveret,
Under the rising moon;

Owl and Newt and Nightjar:
They take their shapes and creep
Silent as churchyard lichen,
While she squats asleep.

All of these dead were stirring:
Each unto each did call,
'A Witch, a Witch is sleeping
Under the churchyard wall;

'A Witch, a Witch is sleeping . . .'
The shrillness ebbed away;
And up the way-worn moon clomb bright,
Hard on the track of day.

She shone, high, wan, and silvery;
Day's colours paled and died:
And, save the mute and creeping worm,
Nought else was there beside.

Names may be writ; and mounds rise;
Purporting, Here be bones:
But empty is that churchyard
Of all save stones.

Owl and Newt and Nightjar,
Leveret, Bat, and Mole
Haunt and call in the twilight
Where she slept, poor soul.

Walter de la Mare

The Ghost's Song

Woe's me! woe's me!
The acorn's not yet
Fallen from the tree
That's to grow the wood,
That's to make the cradle,
That's to rock the bairn,
That's to grow a man,
That's to lay me.

Anon

A Meeting

When George began to climb all unawares
He saw a horrible face at the top of the stairs.

The rats came tumbling down the planks,
Pushing past without a word of thanks.

The rats were thin, the stairs were tall,
But the face at the top was the worst of all.

It wasn't the ghost of his father or mother.
When they are laid there's always another.

It wasn't the ghost of people he knew.
It was worse than this, shall I tell you who?

It was himself, oh what a disgrace.
And soon they were standing face to face.

At first they pretended neither cared
But when they met they stood and stared.

One started to smile and the other to frown,
And one moved up and the other moved down.

But which emerged and which one stays,
Nobody will know till the end of his days.

George D. Painter

Awesome Beasts

The Marrog

My desk's at the back of the class
   And nobody, nobody knows
      I'm a Marrog from Mars
With a body of brass
   And seventeen fingers and toes.

Wouldn't they shriek if they knew
   I've three eyes at the back of my head
      And my hair is bright purple
My nose is deep blue
   And my teeth are half-yellow, half-red.

My five arms are silver, and spiked
   With knives on them sharper than spears.
I could go back right now, if I liked –
   And return in a million light-years.

I could gobble them all,
For I'm seven foot tall
   And I'm breathing green flames from my ears.

Wouldn't they yell if they knew,
   If they guessed that a Marrog was here?
Ha-ha, they haven't a clue –
   Or wouldn't they tremble with fear!
'Look, look, a Marrog'
   They'd all scream – and SMACK
The blackboard would fall and the ceiling would crack
   And teacher would faint, I suppose.
But I grin to myself, sitting right at the back
   And nobody, nobody knows.

                    R. C. Scriven

The Silent Eye

On the moon lives an eye.
It flies about in the sky,
Staring, glaring, or just peering.
You can't see what it uses for steering.
It is about the size of a large owl,
But has no feathers, and so is by no means a fowl.
Sometimes it zips overhead from horizon to horizon
Then you know it has seen something surprisin'.
Mostly it hovers just above you and stares
Rudely down into your most private affairs.
Nobody minds it much, they say it has charm.
It has no mouth or hands, so how could it do harm?
Besides, as I say, it has these appealing ways.
When you are sitting sadly under crushing dismays,
This eye floats up and gazes at you like a mourner,
Then droops and wilts and a huge tear sags from its corner,
And soon it is sobbing and expressing such woe
You begin to wish it would stop it and just go.

Ted Hughes

The Horny Goloch

The horny-goloch is an awesome beast,
Soople an' scaly;
It has two horns, an' a hantle o' feet,
An' a forkie tailie.

Anon

The Mewlips

The shadows where the Mewlips dwell
  Are dark and wet as ink,
And slow and softly rings their bell,
  As in the slime you sink.

You sink into the slime, who dare
  To knock upon their door,
While down the grinning gargoyles stare
  And noisome waters pour.

Beside the rotting river-strand
  The drooping willows weep,
And gloomily the gorcrows stand
  Croaking in their sleep.

Over the Merlock Mountains a long and weary way,
In a mouldy valley where the trees are grey,
By a dark pool's borders without wind or tide,
Moonless and sunless, the Mewlips hide.

The cellars where the Mewlips sit
  Are deep and dank and cold
With single sickly candle lit;
  And there they count their gold.

Their walls are wet, their ceilings drip;
  Their feet upon the floor
Go softly with a squish-flap-flip,
  As they sidle to the door.

They peep out slyly; through a crack
  Their feeling fingers creep,
And when they've finished, in a sack
  Your bones they take to keep.

Beyong the Merlock Mountains, a long and lonely road,
Through the spider-shadows and the marsh of Tode,
And through the wood of hanging trees and the gallows-weed,
You go to find the Mewlips – and the Mewlips feed.

J. R. R. Tolkien

The Hairy Toe

Once there was a woman went out to pick beans,
and she found a Hairy Toe.
She took the Hairy Toe home with her,
and that night, when she went to bed,
the wind began to moan and groan.
Away off in the distance
she seemed to hear a voice crying,
'Where's my Hair-r-ry To-o-oe?
Who's got my Hair-r-ry To-o-oe?'

The woman scrooched down,
'way down under the covers,
and about that time
the wind appeared to hit the house,

smoosh,

and the old house creaked and cracked
like something was trying to get in.
The voice had come nearer,
almost at the door now,
and it said,
'Where's my Hair-r-ry To-o-oe?
Who's got my Hair-r-ry To-o-oe?'

The woman scrooched further down
under the covers
and pulled them tight around her head.

The wind growled around the house
like some big animal
and r-r-um-mbled
over the chimbley.
All at once she heard the door cr-r-a-ack
and Something slipped in
and began to creep over the floor.

The floor went
cre-e-eak, cre-e-eak
at every step that thing took towards her bed.
The woman could almost feel
it bending over her bed.
There in an awful voice it said:
'Where's my Hair-r-ry To-o-oe?
Who's got my Hair-r-ry To-o-oe?
You've got it!'

Traditional American

Charm for the Sleeping Child

Let the superstitious wife
Neer the childs heart lay a knife:
Point be up, and Haft be downe;
(While she gossips in the towne)
This 'mongst other mystick charms
Keeps the sleeping child from harms.

Robert Herrick

Charm for the Stables

Hang up Hooks, and Sheers to scare
Hence the Hag, that rides the Mare,
Till they be all over wet,
With the mire, and the sweat:
This observ'd, the Manes shall be
Of your horses, all knot-free.

Robert Herrick

The Snitterjipe

In mellowy orchards, rich and ripe,
Is found the luminous Snitterjipe.
Bad boys who climb the bulging trees
Feel his sharp breath about their knees;
His trembling whiskers tickle so,
They squeak and squeal till they let go.
They hear his far-from-friendly bark;
They see his eyeballs in the dark
Shining and shifting in their sockets
As round and big as pears in pockets.
They feel his hot and wrinkly hide;
They see his nostrils flaming wide,
His·tapering teeth, his jutting jaws,
His tongue, his tail, his twenty claws.
His hairy shadow in the moon,
It makes them sweat, it makes them swoon;
And as they climb the orchard wall,
They let their pilfered pippins fall.
The Snitterjipe suspends pursuit
And falls upon the fallen fruit;
And while they flee the monster fierce,
Apples, not boys, his talons pierce.
With thumping hearts they hear him munch –
Six apples at a time he'll crunch.
At length he falls asleep, and they
On tiptoe take their homeward way.
But long before the blackbirds pipe
To welcome day, the Snitterjipe
Has fled afar, and on the green
Only his fearsome prints are seen.

James Reeves

A Short Litany

From witches and wizards and longtail'd buzzards,
And creeping things that run in hedge bottoms,
Good Lord deliver us.

Traditional

Index of first lines

Index of authors